WATER PLANET

Life in the
GULF OF
MEXICO

Amie Jane Leavitt

PURPLE TOAD
PUBLISHING

TEXAS

FLORIDA

CUBA

GULF OF MEXICO

MEXICO

Welcome to the Gulf of Mexico! This horseshoe-shaped body of water is found at the bottom of North America. It arches from Mexico to Florida in the United States. At the opening to the Gulf is the dolphin-shaped island of Cuba. All kinds of plants and animals make their home in the Gulf of Mexico. Let's dive in and take a look!

HERE 1475 FT
ABOVE
THE OCEAN
THE MIGHTY
MISSISSIPPI
BEGINS
TO FLOW
ON ITS
WINDING WAY
2552 MILES
TO THE
GULF OF
MEXICO

Thirty-three major rivers drain into the Gulf of Mexico. The Mississippi **(mis-uh-SIP-ee)** River is one of them. Where it enters the Gulf of Mexico, fresh river water mixes with salt water.

Mud from the rivers settles in the Gulf, creating a swampy area called a delta. Grasses, mangroves **(MANG-grohvs)**, and flowering plants grow there. Brown pelicans, herons, egrets **(EE-grets)**, spoonbills, and ibises **(AY-bis-es)** wade along the shore.

The American alligator lurks in the delta, waiting to catch a meal. The diamondback turtle climbs onto land to lay its eggs in the sand.

Snapping gators make their home in the shallow waters of the Mississippi River. The diamonback turtle (right) lives to be about 25 to 40 years old.

Seagrass grows in shallow waters along the coastlines. These plants grow blade-like leaves. Their roots help keep sand from washing away. The plants also help keep the water clear. Many types of sea animals live among these grasses.

The sea robin lives in seagrass on the seafloor. It has spikes on its fins that act like legs. With these special fins, this fish can both swim and walk.

The brown pelican lives along the coastlines. This animal has a big pouched bill used to scoop up fish.

A hare is another name for a rabbit. Scientists named this creature the sea hare because it looks like a rabbit.

The sea hare is a soft-bodied animal that also lives in the seagrass. When it gets scared, it shoots a cloud of dark ink into the water just like a squid.

Manatees (MAN-uh-tees) live along the coasts of the Gulf of Mexico. These large mammals swim in shallow, slow-moving waters. Manatees eat underwater grasses, mangrove leaves, and algae (AL-jee). They can eat up to 600 pounds of food every day.

Manatees can grow to be 12 feet long and weigh 1,500 pounds. Because they look so cuddly, some people call them the teddy bears of the sea. Others call them sea cows. Yet, the manatee isn't a bear or a cow. Its closest relative is actually the elephant!

The manatee's face has wrinkly skin and whiskers. It has two paddle shaped flippers and the same shaped tail.

Sargassum (sar-GAS-um) is a type of golden brown seaweed. It floats in huge, thick mats on the water. The Gulf of Mexico has more sargassum than most of the earth's oceans.

Sargassum is a floating jungle. Crabs, seahorses, tunas, billfish, filefish, sea slugs, and shrimp all live here. Many different types of sea animals begin their life in sargassum. Female fish lay their eggs in the mats. When the eggs hatch, the thick seaweed gives small fish a place to hide.

Seahorses like to swim with a partner. They link their tails together and move as one through the water.

Animals that can camouflage (KAM-uh-flah-shh) or blend in with their environment can hide from other animals.

Some fish live their whole lives in the sargassum. The sargassum fish is one of those. Its frilly fins make it look like seaweed. It can also change its color to blend in with the sargassum. It is a type of frogfish which can hop on top of the seaweed.

Some sealife have spiky (SPY-kee) bodies. These help protect them from being eaten.

Reefs are ridges of rock, sand, or coral in the sea. Some reefs are deep underwater. Some are just below the surface. Others peep up above the waves. Some reefs form from man-made things, too. There are more than 750 known shipwrecks in the Gulf of Mexico. These may form artificial (ar-tuh-FISH-uhl) reefs. Reefs provide a home for many different types of aquatic (uh-KWAH-tik) plants and animals.

Hammerhead sharks' eyes are wide apart, giving them a greater range of vision than other sharks.

Flower Garden Banks is one of the natural reefs in the Gulf of Mexico. It is 100 miles off of the Texas coast. Colorful starfish, spiny sea urchins, smooth sand dollars, and slow-moving sea cucumbers live here. So do hammerhead sharks and stingrays. The bottlenose dolphin also plays in this underwater oasis (oh-AY-sis).

The bottlenose dolphin can live for over 40 years.

At least eight different types of dolphins live in the Gulf of Mexico. There are more Atlantic bottlenose dolphins here than in any other sea. These dolphins are light gray with a pink belly. They have a short nose and a full smile, with 80 to 100 teeth. They eat fish, squid, shrimp, crabs, and lobsters.

Groups of dolphins are called pods. Living in large groups helps keep dolphins safe from predators (PREH-dih-turs).

Many animals like to live in groups. There's safety in numbers.

A sperm whale's brain is about 6 times larger than a human brain.

Minke whales, humpback whales, killer whales, and sperm whales also live in the Gulf of Mexico.

A sperm whale can be up to 65 feet long and weigh about 50 tons. It eats mainly squid, which lives on the seafloor. It eats about one ton of squid every day. It can dive 3,000 feet to get its food. The sperm whale has a huge brain. In fact, it has the largest brain of any animal that has ever lived.

Turn on the heat! Deep in the Gulf of Mexico it is dark and cold. The vampire squid, with its cape-like webbing, feels quite at home here.

It is dark and cold in the deepest part of the Gulf of Mexico. Very little sunlight can reach this part of the sea. As a result, many unusual creatures dwell in this murky place. The vampire squid is one of them. This animal isn't really a squid. It just looks like one. It has huge blue eyes that help it see in the dark. It has eight arms connected by a web. It can turn itself inside out for protection.

Some deep-sea dwellers are like fireflies. They glow in the dark in bright pink, yellow, purple, green, and blue. The glowing light helps these creatures find food and mates. Deep-sea fish, jellyfish, algae, bacteria **(bak-TEER-ee-uh)**, worms, sea stars, and some kinds of sharks can all make their own light.

Some people call these star-shaped creatures "star fish." But they're really not fish at all. So they should be called "sea stars."

Up above near the shore, the Gulf of Mexico's waters are warm and bright. The animals that live here certainly don't need to be able to glow in the dark!

The ibis (EYE-bis) is a bird that spends its days in the gulf's shallow waters. It snatches all kinds of food from its wetland home. It eats fish, insects, reptiles, crabs, and even some kinds of plants.

Whether it's the shallow waters to the deep sea, there are many amazing creatures that call the Gulf of Mexico their home sweet home.

The ibis's long pointed beak lets it dig down into the mud to find food.

FURTHER READING

Books

Hanes, Kathleen. *Seagrass Dreams: A Counting Book.* Lake Forest, CA: Seagrass Press, 2017.

Hoyt, Erich. *Creatures of the Deep.* Buffalo, NY: Firefly Ebooks, 2014.

Marsh, Laura. *National Geographic Readers: Manatees.* Washington, D.C.: National Geographic Children's books, 2014.

Marsh, Laura. *National Geographic Readers: Sea Turtles.* Washington, D.C.: National Geographic Society, 2011.

Marsh, Laura. *National Geographic Readers: Whales.* Washington, D.C.: National Geographic Society, 2011.

Priddy, Roger. *Smart Kids: Coral Reef.* London: Priddy Books, 2014.

Stewart, Melissa. *Dolphins.* Washington, D.C.: National Geographic Children's Books, 2011.

Web Sites

Discovery Kids: Sharks
  http://discoverykids.com/category/sharks/

The Dolphin Research Center: "Manatee Facts for Kids"
  https://www.dolphins.org/kids_manatee_facts

The Florida Museum of Natural History: "Life in Seagrasses"
  https://www.flmnh.ufl.edu/southflorida/habitats/seagrasses/life/

algae (AL-jee)—Small plants that grow in the water.

aquatic (ah-KWAH-tik)—Living in water.

artificial (ar-tuh-FISH-uhl)—Made by humans rather than occurring naturally.

bacteria (bak-TEER-ee-uh)—Very small living things that are made of only one cell.

brackish (BRAK-ish)—Having a mixture of saltwater and freshwater.

delta (DEL-tuh)—A swampy area shaped like a triangle that is formed when a river splits into smaller rivers before it flows into an ocean.

oasis (oh-AY-sis)—A place that provides peace and safety.

predators (PREH-dih-turs)—An animal that hunts other animals for food.

squid (SKWID)—A deep-sea animal that has eight legs plus two longer arms; it can squirt ink to avoid enemies.

INDEX

Printing   1   2   3   4   5   6   7   8   9

The Arctic Ocean
The Atlantic Ocean
The Caribbean
The Gulf of Mexico
The Indian Ocean
The Mediterranean Sea
The Pacific Ocean

ABOUT THE AUTHOR: Amie Jane Leavitt graduated from Brigham Young University and is an accomplished author, researcher, and photographer. She has written more than sixty books for kids, has contributed to online and print media, and has worked as a consultant, writer, and editor for numerous educational publishing and assessment companies. To check out a listing of Amie's current projects and published works, visit her website at www.amiejaneleavitt.com.

Publisher's Cataloging-in-Publication Data
Leavitt, Amie Jane.
   Gulf of Mexico / written by Amie Jane Leavitt.
     p. cm.
Includes bibliographic references, glossary, and index.
ISBN 9781624693670
1. Mexico, Gulf of—Juvenile literature. 2. Marine biology—Mexico, Gulf of—Juvenile literature. I. Series: Water planet.
 F296 2017
 551.463

eBook ISBN: 9781624693687

PURPLE TOAD
PUBLISHING

Library of Congress Control Number: 2017940568